PARRY THOMAS AND PENDINE

By

MARK BERRESFORD

Published on behalf of
THE PENDINE COMMUNITY COUNCIL
by
CONNOR and BUTLER
69 Guildford Road, Colchester, Essex CO1 2RZ.

To Angie, who has had to learn to live, breathe and sleep Parry Thomas, and to the memory of Ivor Williams, late Chairman of Pendine Community Council, who passed away before completion of this book.

Contents

ISBN 0 947699 03 1

Foreword

It was originally intentioned to publish this little booklet as a tribute to the memory of Parry Thomas on the centenary of his birth, which according to all the standard reference books, Hugh Tours' biography and even Thomas's own gravestone agree as being 1885. However, it was pointed out to me by Mr. Owen Wyn-Owen, the man responsible for resurrecting and restoring Thomas's car, 'Babs', that he was in fact born in 1884. On checking with the Registrar of Births, Deaths and Marriages in Thomas's birth place, Wrexham, it was found that Mr. Owen was indeed correct.

It is hoped therefore, that the reader will not object to this book being late; if nothing else, it gives the opportunity to correct the misconception over the date of Thomas's birth.

Betty Ebsworth, daughter of the owners of the Beach Hotel, standing in front of 'Babs' in April 1926. The garage where 'Babs' and Campbell's Bluebird were kept whilst at Pendine was to the left of the photograph – it has long been demolished but the wall in the photograph is still in situ.

(Photograph by courtesy of Mrs. Betty Jones, nee Ebsworth)

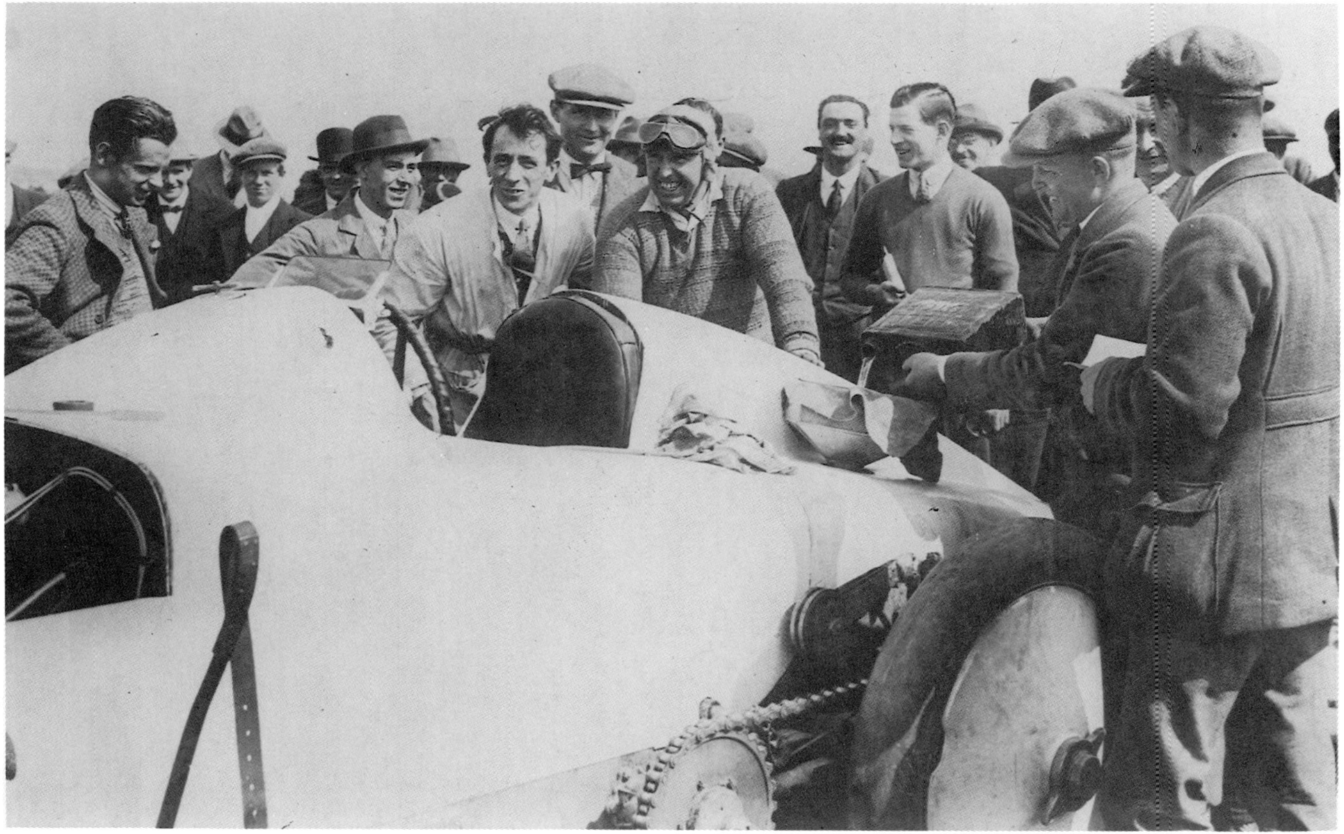

Smiles from Thomas and Ken Taylor on hearing that Thomas and 'Babs' had broken the World's Land Speed Record – April 1926. Note the size of the links of the drive chain.
(Photograph by courtesy of Mrs. Betty Jones, nee Ebsworth)

The Gentle Giant

Parry Thomas is best remembered nowadays because of the the tragic and bizarre circumstances surrounding his death on Pendine Sands in March 1927, and the burial, and subsequent resurrection in 1969 of his giant aero-engined car, 'Babs'. This hardly does credit to the memory of the man , who was without doubt, the most popular and successful British racing driver of his day. Whilst this is how most people remember Thomas, there are many who are of the opinion that he wasted his talents, and eventually his life, by motor racing, and consider him to be one of the most original motor vehicle designers of the century.

To find the true personality of Parry Thomas, one must look at both spheres of his activities, and for anyone wishing to learn the full story, the definitive biography, 'Parry Thomas, Designer-Driver' by Hugh Tours (Published by B.T.Batsford, 1959) is highly recommended, if you are lucky enough to find a copy. For its part, this little booklet is primarily concerned with Thomas's record breaking activities at Pendine in the last three years of his life, but a brief description of Thomas the man, and a resumé of his career, does not seem out of place.

Parry Thomas was a big man, 6'3" tall, of muscular build, well over 13 stone in weight. He had protruding teeth, which he usually covered up with a sullen scowl, and this action was taken by many, particularly pressmen, as a sign of unfriendliness, or downright hostility. In fact he was the warmest and friendliest of men, with a large circle of friends, some of whom had known him since his college days. Despite the fact, or perhaps because of the fact that he never married, he had a great love of children, and children in return loved him; he was a regular fixture at The Schoolboy's Own Exhibition, accompanying 'Babs', and signing autographs for the children.

Away from the steering wheel, he was rather quiet and shy, awkward when in the presence of the opposite sex, but possessing the charm and wit of the Welsh. In a racing car however, he was utterly fearless, a demon who would take cold calculated chances which lesser men would never dream of taking, and the stories are legion of his dare-devil exploits at Brooklands. In one race, whilst overtaking a slower car on the banking, travelling at over 125 miles per hour, he put one wheel of his Leyland-Thomas over the top. On returning to the pits, he calmly went over to the Clerk of the Course, Col. Lindsay Lloyd and suggested that it would be a good idea if a dotted line was painted 10 feet from the top, as a guide for when travelling at speed.

As well as his racing interests, Thomas was also a keen lawn tennis and cricket player, often found at Queen's Club or playing a game of cricket with his cronies at Brooklands. Although he died a bachelor, women seemed to find him irresistible; the famous musical comedy star of the 20's and 30's, 'June' was a regular visitor to Brooklands with her boyfriend the racing driver Woolf 'Babe' Barnato, and she was one of the many women that fell under the spell of the shy Welshman. She recalled in her autobiography, 'The Glass Ladder', (Pub: Heinemann, 1960) the many visits to Thomas's bungalow, built within the circuit; the cracked mugs of strong tea, the copy of 'Autocar' thrust into her hand as 'light reading' and the diffident smile, revealing a row of tobacco stained teeth that looked "as though they had been thrown in from a distance". Thomas must have taken to heart June's pleading for him to have them fixed, for on a subsequent visit, she noticed that when he smiled, there was a pair of enormous white tusks set between their nicotine-stained brethren'. Thomas's embarrassment at June's comments as to how handsome he now looked, can easily be imagined!

The Early Years

John Godfrey Parry Thomas (nobody ever called him John - his close friends all knew him as 'Tommy') was born on Sunday, the 6th April 1884 at 6, Spring Road, in Wrexham, the second of a family of four children. His father, John William Thomas was curate of the local church, and in January 1888, he took up the position of vicar in the little village of Bwlch-y-Cibau, near Oswestry. Whilst still at Oswestry School, he showed great interest in engineering, a career not thought to be in keeping with a vicar's son, but his desire to enter that profession was strong, and in 1902, he went to London to study at the City and Guilds Engineering College, where his interest lay primarily in the field of electrical engineering. It was whilst he was there that he struck up a friendship with Ken Thomson, a student from New Zealand, who was later to become Thomas's assistant in his Brooklands days and who after Thomas's death, became head of Messrs. Thomson and Taylor Ltd., a company which became famous through its work on Malcolm Campbell's various 'Bluebirds' and its high standard of engineering and coachwork,

On leaving college in 1905, Thomas was apprenticed to Messrs. Siemens', later moving on to Clayton and Shuttleworth's, and with the invaluable knowledge gained from his time with these companies, he decided to set up on his own, with financial aid from his parents. He had been experimenting for some time on an electrical transmission of infinitely variable gear ratio, but was unable to find sufficient financial backing, until news of his work reached the ears of Ken Thomson's brother Hedley. He and another partner, W.F.Hickman, came up with the necessary monetary assistance, and in 1908, Thomas found himself co-director of Thomas Transmissions Ltd., with offices in Kensington High Street. Due to the size of the motors and switch-gear required, the idea was only suitable for lorries and other large vehicles, and Thomas simply did not have the funds or equipment to manufacture in his own workshops, so he approached Leyland Motors Ltd. to see if he could have use of their facilities. The results of this partnership included the construction of a London 'bus, railcars for New Zealand and South Africa and a tramcar for Morecambe Corporation, but due to the size and complexity of his invention, weighed against the rapid improvement in diesel engines, and the low price of coal, the Thomas Transmission was left to die a death. In fact his idea was some 70 years ahead of its time, for investigations into a similar system are currently under way, and with modern technology, such an idea is quite feasible.

With the outbreak of the First World War, Thomas was much in demand on Government advisory boards, in the fields of munitions, aero engines and tanks; he even devised plans for an electrically powered airship, larger than any Zeppelin, but nothing came of this scheme. In February 1917, he was offered the position of Chief Engineer at Leyland Motors, and his first task on taking up this job was the design and construction of a new aero engine, a project left unfinished by his predecessor. In true Thomas fashion, the self-willed Welshman scrapped the existing design and set to work on a design of his own, but by the time the prototype had been constructed, the war was virtually over and the whole project was abandoned.

The Lion of Olympia

With the War over, Leyland's soon got back to peacetime lorry production, but a new scheme was under way, the production of the world's finest car, with money no object. The idea of an ultra-luxurious car pre-dated Thomas's appointment as Chief Engineer, when in 1916 it was decided to build a car of V-12 engine configuration based on the American Packard Twin Six. With the arrival on the scene of Thomas, the V-12 design was scrapped, and he conceived a straight eight-cylinder engine, ably assisted by Reid Railton, another engineering genius, whose talents were later put to use by Malcolm Campbell and John Cobb for their record-breaking cars.

The Leyland Eight, as the resulting car was christened, was a magnificent car, brim-full of innovative ideas, and when shown at the 1920 Motor Show it was dubbed, 'The Lion of Olympia'. Many of the features taken for granted on a modern car, such as servo-assisted brakes, anti-roll bars and a variable-rake steering column all first saw light of day on the Leyland Eight. Another innovation was an automatic chassis lubrication system operated by movement of the rear springs. The adjective 'beautiful' is not one which springs to mind when the Leyland Eight is discussed, with its square radiator and enormous conical hub caps, but it was certainly individual - a little touch of Thomas's humour was to be found in the square headlights with round glasses, supposedly modelled on his wristwatch.

To call the car individual is hardly an understatement, for at £2,500 for the chassis alone, it was well out of reach of all but the fantastically wealthy, and in total only fourteen cars were built. Two of the owners were an Indian Maharajah, and Michael Collins, Commander-in-Chief of the Irish Free State. With a slump in the motor trade in the early '20s, the demand for a car costing well over £2,500 was virtually nil, and production ceased in 1922.

It is to be lamented, that no original version of the Leyland Eight survives, however, there does exist a two-seater, cannibalised from bits found in Thomas's workshop after his death by Thomson and Taylor; this car is now in the BL Heritage Collection at Syon Park, London.

A New Career

It is said that every Leyland Eight was personally tested up to 100 mph by Thomas before letting their well-heeled owners take possession, so it hardly came as a surprise to the Leyland directors, when in late 1921 Thomas asked their permission to drive in a race at Brooklands. The directors refused his request, pointing out that

Parry Thomas in characteristic pose at the wheel of the Leyland - Thomas.

Thomas in 'Babs' outside the Beach Hotel, Pendine, October 1925. This was the occasion of Thomas's first record attempt at Pendine.

Malcolm Campbell in the Napier-Campbell 'Bluebird' at Pendine, 2nd of January 1927. Thomas, in leather coat and hat looks on anxiously.

it was hardly right to have the most expensive British car involved in competing with lesser vehicles (this is also true of Rolls Royce, very few ever raced at Brooklands and the ones that did were entered by private individuals) and besides, they could hardly afford to risk their Chief Engineer's neck at anything as reckless as motor racing. After much badgering from Thomas, they agreed to a relatively safe compromise of granting him permission to race, but on the strict understanding that the car ran in full touring rig - the mere spectacle of a fully equipped car lapping at over 90 m.p.h. would be excellent publicity, whether Thomas won or not. What a shock they must have had when on Easter Monday, the 17th of April 1922, Thomas lined up for the start of the 100 m.p.h. Short Handicap, with the Leyland stripped to absolute basics! Whether Thomas was in awe of the great names he was lined up against... Count Zborowski, Kaye Don, Henry Segrave and Malcolm Campbell, or whether the excitement of lining up for the start of his first race in front of thousands of spectators unnerved him will never be known, for when the starting flag dropped, he slipped the Leyland's clutch and was left standing, an inauspicious start to his racing career.

It must be pointed out that racing at Brooklands bore little resemblance to modern motor racing, with its various formula classifications. Throughout Brooklands' history, races were mostly run on a handicap system, with the smaller, slower cars given as much as a lap start from the giant aero-engined cars then prevalent, such as Count Zborowski's 23,092 c.c. chain-driven monster 'Chitty-Bang-Bang'. It was therefore a common sight to see a racing-bodied Austin Seven racing against one of Zborowski's creations. If that was not complicated enough, the performance of the driver was taken into consideration, a throw-back to when motor racing was run on the lines of horse racing.

After an ignominious first meeting, Thomas soon improved and by his third outing had chalked up his first of many wins. Not one to rest on his laurels, Thomas almost immediately set about improving the racing Leyland, a two-seater 'Speed Model' and by July 1922 had fitted a new body with a pointed tail, whilst the engine compartment was totally enclosed in a streamlined front end, leaving the huge Leyland radiator sitting incongruously isolated at the front. The original bright aluminium body was painted white, with the chassis and wheels in pale blue; this colour scheme was applied to all of Thomas's cars until his death. With the improved Leyland, Thomas managed to gain 3 wins in the last four race meetings of 1922, and was placed 8 times, a fine result for a first season of racing.

Even at this early stage in his racing career, Thomas was already thinking about record breaking, and with the closure of the track to competitive racing, was out to attempt to break existing records for the class of car (cars with engines not exceeding 7784c.c.). On Thursday the 9th of November 1922 he took the World's Record for the 10 miles flying start, at 114.74 m.p.h. So 1922 closed with Thomas well pleased with his first season.

The Hermit of Brooklands

By 1923 the Leyland directors were becoming increasingly alarmed by the amount of time spent by their Chief Engineer at Brooklands, and after the inevitable ultimatum, Thomas's contract was mutually terminated. After this, he set up home in 'The Hermitage', which was a bungalow within the track itself. This he shared with his old friend Ken Thomson, who was now second in command of the small workforce which Thomas had gathered around him, and also his two alsatians, Togo and Bess.

Thomas was already gaining the reputation of being a daring and resourceful driver, driving high up on the steeply banked track, sometimes within a couple of inches of the edge, earning himself the nickname in the press 'Daredevil Thomas'. Another, far less complimentary nickname was 'The Hermit of Brooklands', on account of his ascetic lifestyle, and indifference, bordering on rudeness, towards certain pressmen. None of this mattered to Thomas, as now being his own boss, he could devote all of his time to improving his existing car, and designing new ones. His first job was a collaboration to produce a racing version of the Marlborough car, a French import, which he re-engined with a unit of his own design, and marketed as the Marlborough-Thomas. Although this car did not live up to Thomas's expectations on the track, he eventually designed a single-seat racing car based on the Marlborough-Thomas, and with this he achieved some notable successes.

1923 proved to be a good year for Thomas and the big Leyland, winning eight races outright at Brooklands, as well as taking the 5 and 10 mile flying start World Records at 119.43 and 116.25 m.p.h. respectively.

The winter of 1923 saw Thomas working on his most ambitious project taken on since setting up on his own, the rebuilding and rebodying of the Leyland. What emerged from his workshop bore little resemblance to the Leyland Eight. The Leyland-Thomas, as the car was christened, had been lowered in height and fitted with a long, streamlined body, finishing in a downward sweep to a long pointed tail. The driver's seat was offset to the right, with a streamlined 'hump' fore and aft, and provision was also made for a passenger seat lower than the driver's position, but this was usually covered over. In fact Thomas was one of the true pioneers of motor car streamlining, and a look at photographs of other racing cars of the time show just how radical Thomas's design was. An obvious aid to getting a few more miles per hour out of the car was the scrapping of the enormous square radiator and its substitution with an inclined one, totally encased with a streamlined cowling. The body work aside, much was done to improve the efficiency of the engine and to this end, a new crankshaft and con rods were designed, and petrol was now fed to the cylinders via four Zenith carburettors.

The work on the Leyland-Thomas dragged on into the 1924 season, so Thomas had to look around for a car to race. His friend, Lionel Rapson, head of Rapson Tyres, had purchased a Lanchester Forty, with the intention of using it for high speed tyre testing, a science then very much in its infancy, and for the first meeting of the year, this was the car Thomas used. Thomas was to be associated on and off with the Lanchester for the rest of his career, securing some notable wins.

By May 1924, the Leyland-Thomas was ready, so Thomas decided to go for more records, and on Thursday the 22nd of May took the flying start World's Records for 5 and 10 mile distances at 122.86 and 120.46 m.p.h. respectively. Not content with this, and knowing full well that the Leyland-Thomas was capable of even greater speed, he was out again on Thursday the 26th of June, when he broke the World's Land Speed Record, then known as the Flying Mile, at 129.73 m.p.h., snatching the record by a fraction of a second from K. Lee Guinness. This record run necessitated a two-way run round the Brooklands track; the track was not designed for clockwise running, and such a feat was quite dangerous due to the layout of parts of the circuit. This was the last time the Land Speed Record was broken on a racing track; however the record did not last long, for on the 12th of July, Ernest Eldridge in his 21,714 c.c. Fiat 'Mephistopheles' averaged 145.89 m.p.h. on a public road at Arpajon, in France.

Thomas himself was in France in August, for a speed test and hill climb at Boulogne, and carried off the fastest time of the day, in spite of stiff competition. Two important developments were taking place in France at this time; one was the opening of a very fast, banked racing circuit at Linas-Montlhery in October, the other was the reports of a car being built expressly for taking the Land Speed

Record. The backer of this venture was an Egyptian gambler, Prince Djelaleddin, to whom money was no object, and the designer was one M. Moglia, an Italian with a considerable reputation. The car was quickly nicknamed 'Djelmo', a corruption of the two names. Thomas was well aware that in 'Djelmo' he would have stiff opposition in regaining the Land Speed Record, but already a more imminent threat was on the horizon.

Pendine

The little village of Pendine, in the county of Carmarthenshire, had long been famous for its expanse of clean, flat sand, and ever since the invention of the petrol engine, people had come along to drive or ride along the sands and indeed, motor cycle races had been held there since the early 1920s. In 1924, the R.A.C. organised a Six Day's Trial in Wales, and the opportunity was taken for officials to survey the sands between Pendine and Laugharne, with a view to using them for short-distance speed record attempts. Once they had been approved, the first man to attempt the Land Speed Record on Pendine Sands was a speed king who made his name at Brooklands-Malcolm Campbell. Campbell, then 39 years old (slightly younger than Thomas) had been on the racing scene since 1907, when he raced a motorcycle at the very first Brooklands meeting, and by 1924, he had established himself as one of the most successful racing drivers, and he was certainly the most business-minded.

In 1924 Campbell found himself in the position of being able to buy one of the most powerful and successful racing cars in Britain, K.Lee Guinness's 18,322 c.c. V-12 engined Sunbeam, a car which had already held the World's Land Speed Record at 129.17 m.p.h. It is worth noting here that the international rules on record breaking were in a hopeless muddle at the time. European records were ratified by the Association International des Automobile Clubs Reconnus, and they recognised Guinness as the holder of the Land Speed Record or Flying Mile. In the U.S.A., records were ratified by the American Automobile Association. Their record holder was Tommy Milton, who in April 1920 took his Duesenberg to 156 m.p.h. at Daytona Beach, although this was only a one way run. Needless to say, the A.I.A.C.R. refused to recognise the A.A.A.'s record and vice versa. This was because the A.I.A.C.R. only recognised the principal motoring organisation of any country. In America, this was the Automobile

Club of America, however, this body had no control over motor sports. It was common knowledge that Daytona Beach afforded the best conditions then available for record breaking, but because of the absence of dialogue between the two organisations, it was not possible for Europeans to use Daytona and have their record recognised in Europe.

Campbell, after a disastrous attempt at the record at Fanöe Island, Denmark, during which he shed a tyre at speed, which killed a spectator, decided to try his luck at Pendine, and in September 1924, took the Sunbeam down to see what it could do. His first attempt was marred by bad luck - the weather was poor, and the beach was littered with debris, whilst below the beach surface, a number of drainage culverts ran out to sea, causing some terrible patches of soft sand. Undeterred, he went out the following day, Thursday the 25th of September 1924, and took the mile record at 146.16 m.p.h.

Thomas must have looked on Campbell's achievement with admiration, tinged with not a little envy, knowing full well that the Leyland-Thomas was incapable of breaking, or even remotely equalling Campbell's fine effort. Fate, however, was to take a hand in the proceedings.

'Babs'

The whole of the motoring world was stunned by the news of the death of Count Zborowski at Monza, on the 19th of October 1924, whilst driving in the Italian Grand Prix. Thomas must have felt the loss of this most colourful of racing personalities deeply, for he was a good friend and rival, and he was no doubt interested to learn of the sale of his estate. His eye fell on Zborowski's Higham Special, a monstrous 27,059 c.c. Liberty aero-engined, chain driven car, built for him by his close friend and engineering advisor, Clive Gallop. The car was based on a rather flimsy-looking Rubery Owen frame, the gear box (which the Count wrecked on his first attempt at driving the car, and had to send Gallop by 'plane to Mannheim to obtain the last one in stock) had come from a 1908 Benz, and a Zeppelin-shaped body was fitted by Blythe Brothers of Canterbury, a firm in which Zborowski had an interest. Though sounding a hotch-potch, the car was powerful, developing over 600 h.p., and Zborowski had already put her through her paces, lapping at over 116 m.p.h. at Brooklands. Thomas saw in the Higham Special a cheap way of taking a crack at Campbell's record, and reputedly bought her for £125.

Much speculation has been made as to how the Higham Special came to be known as 'Babs', whether Thomas named her after a lady friend, or a young niece, or whatever. Thomas's own story was that when the car arrived at his Brooklands workshops, one of his mechanics chalked the word 'Baby' on the engine and, amused by this, he decided to keep the name. A great deal of work had to be done on 'Babs', and Thomas was eventually to virtually rebuild the car. He replaced the two original carburettors with four Zenith carburettors, one at each end of the twin inlet manifolds and replaced the original pistons with ones of his own design. He also designed a new multi-plate clutch and aside from the engine, replaced the rather dated and dangerous Mercedes front axle with one from a Leyland Eight, and fitted a streamlined cowl over the radiator.

Work on 'Babs' came to an abrupt end in August 1925, when Thomas crashed the Leyland-Thomas, writing it off. The accident occurred at the Boulogne Speed Trials, when during a practice run, the car went into a skid at high speed on a wet road, and ran backwards into a tree, the impact being so great that the propellor shaft was pushed forward, destroying the engine. Thomas would have to wait until May 1926 before he could race the Leyland-Thomas again, and for the rest of 1925 and early 1926, he had to use 'Babs' or Rapson's Lanchester for races.

Luckily, sufficient work had been done on 'Babs' before the accident occurred with the Leyland-Thomas, so that Thomas could consider taking her to Pendine for a crack at Campbell's record. On the 19th of October, Thomas and his entourage of mechanics left Brooklands for Pendine. Arriving at Pendine, Thomas booked into the Beach Hotel, then run by the Ebsworth family, and after discussions with the R.A.C. timing officials, proceeded to have the course marked out and 'Babs' prepared. Alas, the weather was not on Thomas's side, and after three days of attempts at running 'Babs' at speed on the sands, a task hampered further by a waterlogged beach, packed his bags, loaded 'Babs' back onto her trailer and returned to Brooklands.

The Race To 175 m.p.h.

Malcolm Campbell was already becoming Britain's best known record breaker, having returned to Pendine in July 1925, when he broke his old record for the mile at 150.766 m.p.h., but he knew that the Sunbeam had had its day and that it was time to look for a new car. To this end he

Thomas in 'Babs' at Brooklands, 1927. This photograph shows 'Babs' in her final form, with streamlined fairings encasing the driving chains, and with half of the radiator cowling blanked off to assist in warming the engine up to operating temperature in cold weather.

Babs shows her paces at Pendine, April 1926.

(Top): Thomas and 'Babs' are shown being pushed off on the run back to Pendine. Note that Thomas is wearing one of his famous Fair Isle sweaters - a far cry from the anonymity of modern racing garb! The man in the white overalls is Thomas's Chief Mechanic, Ken Taylor, with whom he had previously worked at Leylands.

(Bottom): 'Babs' travelling through the measured mile at over 170 m.p.h.

Thomas, tired and unwell, forces a smile for the cameras at Pendine on the 3rd of March 1927. Shortly after this photograph was taken, Thomas was tragically killed in circumstances that will never be fully resolved.

commissioned Amherst Villiers, a well-known engineer, to design a new car, sufficiently powerful to reach 175 m.p.h. The engine unit Villiers chose for the job was a 450 h.p. Napier Lion aero-engine, the whole project being rumoured to cost Campbell £10,000 of his own money.

Meanwhile, into the fray came another well-known name, Henry Segrave, who was to drive a supercharged car built by the brilliant Frenchman, Louis Coatalen, Chief Engineer of Sunbeam. Segrave had built up a considerable reputation for himself in a relatively short time; after talking his way into the 1921 Talbot-Darracq team, won for them the first 200 mile race held in Britain, and was successful in Grand Prix races on the Continent. Segrave was chosen by Capt. J.S. Irving, head of the Sunbeam racing team, to take the new car, a relatively small machine of 3978 c.c., and weighing only 18 cwt., not to Pendine, but Southport in Lancashire. The beach there was not as trouble-free as Pendine, having periods of adverse tide and wind conditions, but it afforded a run of some 7 miles, against Pendine's 5 miles. The first runs of the car were unsuccessful, due to sand getting into the supercharger unit. This problem was eventually sorted out, and on the next run all went well until the car hit a bump, leapt into the air, and before Segrave could take his foot off the accelerator, the engine revs leapt up so high that the supercharger was totally wrecked. Luckily, Segrave had passed the kilometre timing strip before the incident, and his average speed for this distance was 152.33 m.p.h., a new record.

Thomas had spent the winter of 1925 working on the Leyland-Thomas and on 'Babs', and the latter now sported a new, streamlined body, starting from a curved cowl, which encased a new inclined radiator and the front dumb irons, and finishing in a long, pointed tail. The driving position was offset to the right, with a hump to the front and rear, as on the Leyland-Thomas, in fact, 'Babs' new body bore a remarkable similarity to the latter.

April 1926 saw 'Babs' ready for another trip to Pendine, and this time the whole venture was professionally organised, with much publicity. Shell-Mex financed the attempt, and paid for 'Babs' to be transported from her Brooklands home to Pendine. Local young men were drafted in to assist in marking the course and in all, 53 people had jobs to do, under the command of Lt. Cdr. Mackenzie-Grieve. As usual, Col. Lindsay-Lloyd was on hand to take charge of the timekeeping arrangements on behalf of the R.A.C.

On Tuesday, the 27th of April, operations began in earnest, and after a couple of warm-up runs, Thomas took the flying mile record at 168.074 m.p.h., and the kilometre record at 169.238 m.p.h., smashing Campbell's mile record by the then phenomenal margin of 16 m.p.h. Though obviously elated with the result, Thomas knew that 'Babs' could be tuned further, for the car had been misfiring, and making black smoke all day. Therefore, after spending some hours adjusting the carburettors, he was out the following day, and managed to push the records up even higher. On this occasion, the mean speeds were 170.624 for the mile, and 171.09 for the kilometre. Disaster almost struck on the second run, when, at high speed, Thomas suddenly slowed down and stopped by the timekeepers' box. On inspecting the car, he was horrified to discover that a nut securing one of the shock absorbers was so loose that it came off at the touch of a hand.

Mindful of the advertising potential, Shell organised a run using ordinary grade petrol instead of 'Babs' usual mixture of 60% aviation fuel and 40% benzole. The R.A.C. supervised the purchasing of the ordinary grade petrol, sealing the tins , and also the filling of 'Babs' fuel tank in her garage beside the Beach Hotel. The runs using the standard grade fuel were not as fast as the record speeds, but still easily beat Campbell's previous record. On the following day, a full page advertisement appeared in The Times:- "Smash! goes the World's Speed Record...Hitherto it has been assumed that racing cars had to have special oils and fuels to stand up to the terrific strain of miles-per-minute. In this remarkable performance Mr. Thomas used standard grades of Shell Motor Oil and Shell Petrol - exactly the same as offered everywhere to the public."

Thomas was the hero of the hour, and praise for his marvellous effort poured in from all quarters, including Malcolm Campbell and Prince Djelaleddin, the latter adding the sniping comment that 'Djelmo' was more than a match for 'Babs'. By way of relief to Thomas's hazardous activities, the following month found him driving a London 'bus during the General Strike, much to the amusement of passengers and passers-by, who recognised the burly Welshman.

The Flying Celt

Thomas's workshop was a hive of activity in 1926; 'Babs' was continually being improved, the wrecked Leyland-Thomas was reconstructed, and work was well advanced on two 1500 c.c. 8 cylinder cars, to be known as the 'Thomas Specials'. They were built with Grand Prix racing in mind, and like 'Babs', bore a remarkable resemblance to the Leyland-Thomas. The distinguishing feature of the Thomas Specials was the low-slung frame, giving a ground clearance of only 5", hence their nickname of the 'flat irons'. The gearbox was most unusual, inasmuch that instead of the normal H-shaped gate, an X-shaped gate was used, necessitating a diagonal pass through the gate from 1st to 2nd gear. Thomas, a most idiosyncratic designer, probably constructed it this way to facilitate a quick change from 1st to 4th gear. Another of his unorthodox ideas was that the handbrake pushed on, rather than pulled.

It was hoped that the two specials, one fitted with a Roots supercharger, and the other unsupercharged, would race in the first British Grand Prix in August 1926, but gearbox trouble prevented them from appearing. The 'flat irons' were never fully developed in Thomas's lifetime, and in fact he won only one race in them. However, after his death, they were raced very successfully by Harold Purdy and R.J. Munday. The latter subsequently removed the Thomas-designed engine, replacing it with a 2700 c.c. Perkins diesel unit, and in this form it took the World's Record for the flying kilometre using a compression engine, at a speed of 94.7 mph.

Thomas was in France with the Leyland-Thomas again in August 1926 for the Boulogne Speed Trials, and although he was reasonably happy with a second place to Segrave's Sunbeam, the day ended in tragedy, when his close personal friend Dick Howey was killed when his Ballot car hit a tree. Two spectators also died, whilst several others were injured, and the meeting was abandoned. Thomas travelled back on the ship which carried Howey's body and the wreckage of his car, the latter being cast into the sea in mid-Channel.

Thomas made his final appearance in a race at Brooklands, on Saturday the 2nd of October, 1926, and fortunately for posterity he had a very successful day. His first win came in the Leyland-Thomas, when he won the Essex Senior Long Handicap at an average 118.96 m.p.h., beating John Cobb (another name later to be associated with the Land Speed Record). The final meeting of the day, the Essex 50 Miles Handicap, was fittingly won by Thomas driving one of the 'flat iron' Thomas Specials. Starting some 8 minutes 33 seconds after the limit man, A.B.Elford in his 1074 c.c. Amilcar, Thomas slowly worked through the field, 'til by lap 15 he was in third place. Lap 18 saw Thomas at the front, and he finished the race a mile ahead of his nearest rival, his average speed being 106.19 m.p.h.

Although racing had finished for the year at Brooklands, Thomas was still busy record breaking, and on Thursday the 7th of October, he took the World's Records for 500 kilometres, 500 miles, and the 3 hours run, using the trusty old Leyland-Thomas. Thomas was out again on the following Thursday, this time behind the wheel of 'Babs', securing class records for 5 and 10 miles, and 10 kilometres. The Leyland-Thomas was out yet again the following Thursday, when Thomas decided to have a crack at the World's Hour Record. The first run in the morning was marred by the Leyland cutting out, but after attention back at the workshop, Thomas was out again in the afternoon. Apart from tyre trouble, the run was incident-free, and the record held by the French driver Ortmans easily fell. In one hour, Thomas had travelled 121 miles, 1307 yards, the average speed being 121.74 m.p.h. If all this reckless record-breaking activity was not enough, Thomas was out yet again on Saturday the 30th of October, this time in the Thomas Special, the target being the 1500 c.c. Hour Record. Needless to say, the old record fell easily, Thomas's average speed being 112.77 m.p.h.

The Last Year

The end of 1926 saw more activity towards record breaking than ever before - Campbell's new Napier-engined 'Bluebird' was now complete, but he was well aware that he would be hard pushed to get above 175 m.p.h. Over in France, work was well advanced on 'Djelmo', which would be making its appearance at Pendine in 1927, however, a much more interesting development was occurring nearer home, in Wolverhampton. Louis Coatalen, Sunbeam's Chief Engineer, was working on building the most powerful car the world had yet seen, and once again, Segrave had been chosen to drive her. The new car was powered by two 22,444 c.c. 12-cylinder Sunbeam aero engines, mounted fore and aft of the driver's cockpit, and they developed a total 1000 h.p. Like 'Babs', and rather unusually for such a modern car, the Sunbeam was chain driven, but even so, Coatalen was confident that speeds in excess of 200 m.p.h. were feasible.

The biggest problem that faced the Sunbeam team was not the car, but where to run her. It was apparent that the 5 miles of beach between Pendine and Laugharne was totally inadequate for a 200 m.p.h. run, and a site out of Britain would be needed. Daytona Beach, in Florida, U.S.A. was the obvious choice, affording a 23 mile run, 10 miles of which were suitable for very high speed, but the fly in the ointment was the lack of discourse between the A.I.A.C.R. and the American Automobile Association, who, it will be remembered, controlled motor sport in America. As neither party recognised the other's records, there was little point in Segrave breaking the record in America if it was not recognised in his own country. The process of reconciliation began in 1925, when the A.I.A.C.R. decided that any national motor organisation represented in their body could delegate control of motor sport and record attempts to another organisation. Thus the Automobile Club of America could delegate these powers to the A.A.A. and bring America into line with Europe. However, this agreement was not immediately acted upon, and the Sunbeam team had to send out frantic telegrams, inducing the two American organisations to come into line as soon as possible. The final agreement came through by the end of 1926, and all that remained was for the A.I.A.C.R. to approve the American electronic timing apparatus.

Meanwhile, Campbell was down at Pendine for Christmas 1926 with the new 'Bluebird', but the car was untested, having never been run on the road or race track. Thomas, ever interested in his great rival's activities, left Brooklands and motored down to Pendine to see the first run of the new car. 'Bluebird' was brought onto the beach on Sunday the 2nd of January 1927, where it became immediately apparent that all was not well. On the first short trial run, Campbell experienced trouble with the gearbox, and to make matters worse, the beach was waterlogged, and the car began to sink in the sand. With the car placed on duckboards, Thomas and Campbell discussed what could be done, and all that night Campbell's team of mechanics, led by Leo Villa, worked on the gearbox. Next day the car was again brought down the ramp onto the beach, but still Campbell could not engage top gear, so deeply disappointed, he returned to his workshops.

The tenacious Malcolm Campbell was back at Pendine on Saturday the 22nd of January, but to no avail; on one run a tyre burst, and later on, he hit one of the patches of soft sand for which Pendine was notorious, taking one of the marking posts on the way. Tidal conditions prevented any further attempts until Friday the 4th of February, when the weather and tides were ideally suited for an attempt at seriously opening up the Napier Lion engine. This time the 'Bluebird' did all that was expected of her, and Thomas's record fell; the mean speeds of the two-way run were 174.223 m.p.h. for the mile and 174.883 m.p.h. for the kilometre.

Thomas was well aware that with the improvements made on 'Babs' over the winter, she was capable of even higher speeds, and it was not beyond the realms of possibility that he could be the first man to reach three miles a minute. Whether he seriously considered 200 m.p.h., (the speed Segrave was aiming for) a possibility is not known, but he organised a series of runs at Pendine, beginning on Monday the 14th of February 1927, well in advance of Segrave's attempt at Daytona, due to be held at the end of March. However a bad attack of influenza, probably brought on by his trip to Pendine in January, prevented him from making the attempt.

With the news that Campbell was planning to try and break his own record before Segrave's run, it was obvious that time was running out for Thomas to have a crack at the record, and even though he was far from well, he organised the teams of mechanics, R.A.C. officials and timekeepers and the small army of assistants provided by Dunlop and Shell-Mex, to be down at Pendine for three days, commencing on Tuesday the 1st of March, which was incidentally, the day Segrave sailed for America.

A Life For Speed

Times Editorial Headline 4th of March 1927.

Thomas motored down to Pendine and put up with the Ebsworths at the Beach Hotel on Monday, the 28th of February. 'Babs' was brought down by trailer from her Brooklands home, and was wheeled into the garage adjoining the hotel. (This garage has since been demolished, but the line of its foundations can be seen at the east end of the hotel's car park, near the steps leading up to the main road.) The weather was rather poor, and it was obvious that Thomas was far from well, since he spent a lot of time in bed. However, he was intent on carrying out his plans, and paid no heed to the remonstrations of his doctor or his friends. In fact he told a reporter that he didn't realise how ill he felt until he had driven a few miles, when he considered abandoning the journey to Pendine, and putting up for the night in Oxford.

Tuesday, the 1st of March was spent examining the state of the beach, but the conditions prevented any attempts to bring 'Babs' down the ramp for a run. Wednesday was no better, so Thomas took the opportunity to rest in bed. Thomas woke on Thursday the 3rd, to find that the weather had improved, and he was soon busy organising the runs for later in the day. A small army of assistants were on hand; Thomas's staff, led by Leslie Callingham, the R.A.C. staff under Lt.Cdr.Mackenzie-Grieve, Col.Lindsay-Lloyd (a strict, but fair individual, still remembered by the older inhabitants of Pendine) and his timekeeping staff, the Dunlop and Shell teams, gangs of local men drafted in to mark the course ,and, last but not least, the press and newsreel cameramen.

The newspaper reports of the events all mentioned that Thomas

Two hitherto unpublished photographs of Thomas at Pendine in March 1927.
(Left) Thomas gives Betty Ebsworth a hug outside the Beach Hotel.
(Right) Thomas with Betty's Uncle, Jack Ebsworth, on the main Street at Pendine.
Photographs kindly provided by Mrs. Betty Jones nee Ebsworth.

Pendine, 3rd March 1927. The mangled wreck of 'Babs' lies where she came to rest.

A wartime production Fordson tractor tows the remains of 'Babs' to the hole that was to be her grave for 42 years.

looked ill and worn-out, but he had told reporters that the weather was so delightful, he could not resist the opportunity of an attempt at the record. Undoubtedly, the true reason for going out on the Thursday was that he knew it would be his last chance to have an attempt at the record, before it was taken out of his reach by Segrave; also, this being the last day he had arranged to be at Pendine, he didn't want to disappoint the spectators and the pressmen.

At about 12.30pm, Thomas brought 'Babs' out of the garage, and ran her down the ramp onto the beach; shortly before that however, Betty Ebsworth, then a teenager, presented Thomas with a lucky black cat doll mascot. In true Thomas style, and bearing in mind his background he refused it, saying "Thank you, but I put not my trust in false gods".

'Babs' was warmed up, and a trial run along the beach was made, but she was making black smoke, and work was obviously needed before an attempt at the record could be made. After attention at the garage, Thomas was off again, and this time the timekeepers were in position. However, although the run was fast, it was not fast enough to break the record. As the car was turned for the return run to Pendine, Thomas said to one of the assistants that he was going back to make further adjustments, and he would be back in about half an hour. Back at Pendine, he changed the specially-made K.L.G. spark plugs, and reset the carburettors, and within twenty minutes he was off again up the beach.

'Babs' was now travelling at great speed, and she was about 100 yards clear of the end of the measured mile (about three miles from the Beach Hotel) when the car was seen to skid, run for 200 yards or so, roll over and slither along upside down, right herself, and run along on three wheels in a great left hand turn, and finally stop facing the sea. Once stationary, 'Babs' engine caught fire, sending a pall of smoke into the cold March sky. Leslie Callingham and one of Thomas's mechanics, Harold 'Jock' Pullen were the first to reach the scene. Although the'Times' report of the inquest stated that both men were standing opposite the timing box when the accident happened, some sources said that they were travelling up the course in Callingham's Bentley. When they arrived at the scene, they were horrified to find Thomas half hanging out of the car, his head severed from the nape of the neck to the forehead. His body was wedged in the car, and flames from the engine fire were already burning his shoes. Pullen and Callingham, still in shock over the sight of their dead boss and friend, bravely risked their own lives to pull the body out of the wreckage, having to break Thomas's legs before they could extricate him. Having finally freed him, and with Pullen receiving serious hand burns in the process, they laid his body on the sand next to the car, and threw a coat over it. By the time the cameras, pressmen and police arrived, the fire had been extinguished, and all that remained to be done, was to remove Thomas's body, and tow the wreckage back to Pendine, The body was placed on a motor tender, and was slowly driven back to the Beach Hotel, where it was laid in the hall adjacent to the garage where Thomas had spent so many hours working on his beloved 'Babs'. 'Babs' herself was hitched to the back of a tractor, and towed back to Pendine, where she was unceremoniously dumped at the bottom of thc ramp, being later towed to the yard at the rear of the Beach Hotel.

The following day an inquest was held, presided over by Dr. Roland Thomas, Coroner for West Carmarthenshire. Evidence was given by Pullen, Callingham, Mr. Gregory, Chief Engineer representing the R.A.C. and Dr. Alexander Lindsay, who had come down from Carmarthen to act on behalf of the R.A.C. as official doctor for the record attempt, and who was on the scene of the accident shortly after it occurred. Callingham commended the actions of Pullen for his noble example in pulling Thomas's body from the blazing wreck, knowing that the petrol tank was liable to explode at any moment. In his evidence to the court, he stated that it was his opinion that the chain must have picked up a pebble in its links, which when run over the teeth of the sprocket wheel, caused the chain to snap, hitting Thomas in the head. Dr. Lindsay, in his evidence said that he was in no doubt that Thomas was killed at the very onset of the trouble, his findings being based on the fact that a piece of Thomas's skull was found at the site of the first skid. Pullen was questioned as to the safety of 'Babs', and whether it was adequately prepared, to which he replied that it had been thoroughly examined before the run, and was in as perfect condition as a mechanic could leave it in, a statement backed up by Mr. Gregory. Gregory also said that it was his opinion that Thomas had heard something was wrong, and had leant over to see, when the chain hit him.

Dr. Thomas recorded a verdict of Accidental Death, and that Mr. Parry Thomas died from injuries to the head as the result of a motor accident. He added that he found nearly the whole of the skull severed from the base, and that death was instantaneous, Thomas suffering no pain.

The true cause of the accident will never be resolved; whenever the name of Parry Thomas is mentioned, people will argue over the cause, but of all the people who have expounded their theories, it is Reid Railton, Thomas's friend and collaborator, and one of the great motor engineers, who seems to offer the most satisfactory explanation as to the cause. He arrived at Pendine about an hour after the accident had occurred, and although he was deeply upset at the death of his friend, he was not as emotionally involved as those who were present. When he examined the offside sprocket wheel leading from the gearbox, which drove the rear wheels by chain, he found a dent in one of the teeth. Having deduced that this could only have been caused by harder steel than that which the sprocket was made of, he discovered that the only harder steel used was for the wheel spokes. Testing a spoke in the dent, he found it fitted perfectly. He deduced that the offside rear wheel had collapsed, throwing one of the spokes into the drive sprocket wheel, and breaking the chain. With the rear wheel missing, the car would have heeled over, and bearing in mind that Thomas was not strapped into the car, he would have been thrown to the right, where he caught the full force of the chain. Blood spattered on the rear of the car seems to substantiate this theory.

The inquest over, the next decision to be made was what was to be done with the remains of 'Babs'. The original idea was to tow her back to the scene of the accident, and leave her to the mercy of the waves, but this scheme was scrapped. It was then decided to bury 'Babs' in the dunes, not far from the village. A large hole was dug, but this soon filled with water, so another hole was dug, a little inland from the dunes. A Fordson tractor towed the wrecked car to the hole, and after a few photographs were taken to record the occasion, Thomas's grieved mechanics and friends pushed her in, along with Thomas's coat and leather driving helmet.

Thomas's body was taken to Brooklands, where it lay in 'The Hermitage'. A private service was held in the bungalow on Monday the 7th of March, attended by his mother, close relatives, Ken Thomson and Thomas's housekeeper and her husband. After the service, the cortege, including six cars laden with wreaths, made their way to St. Mary's Church, Byfleet, whilst overhead, aeroplanes saluted their brother speed king. The church was packed with many friends and employees from Brooklands, some still in their overalls, and after a simple service, Thomas's body was laid to rest, buried with his racing goggles. His grave is marked with a large granite stone, faced with a black cross, and with an inscription that perpetuates the misconception that he was born in 1885.

The Aftermath

It is interesting to speculate on the direction Thomas would have taken had he lived. The most ironic of the jobs on his drawing board was the conversion of 'Babs' from chain to shaft drive, but there were a number of other interesting projects in hand, including continuing work on the 'flat irons', and building a 750 c.c. car, which showed Thomas's gradual move to smaller cars. Earlier in the year, he had bought 'Babe', Barnato's 3-litre Bentley, and a 9 h.p. Riley. One can assume that these would have been a regular sight at Brooklands, however, the most unusual development undoubtedly would have been the building of a power boat. In fact he was to have raced in the Duke of York's Trophy race between Mortlake and Putney in June 1926, but this never materialised.

As mentioned earlier, with his death, Thomas's work at Brooklands was carried on by Ken Thomson, and Thomas's foreman Ken Taylor, and the company survives to the present day, now in nearby Cobham.

As a postscript to the tragedy at Pendine, and to show the futility of Thomas's attempt, Segrave, after careful checking of his own car's driving chains, achieved his wish to be the first man to travel at 200 m.p.h. on land, at Daytona, on the 29th of March 1927, where his mean speed for the mile was 203.79 m.p.h.

Pendine had not yet seen the end of record attempts; 'Djelmo' finally arrived in the Summer of 1927, along with its driver, Giulio Foresti, and his beautiful wife. Foresti spent several weeks working on the car, knowing that Segrave's speed was beyond his grasp, but he could take the British Land Speed Record, for the fastest speed recorded on these shores, for what it was worth. He was finally ready in October, when on a timed run at over 150 m.p.h., the little car somersaulted and threw Foresti out, the friction of hitting the sand removing practically all of his hair. Amazed onlookers gasped when the little Italian got up and walked away, only to collapse in the arms of his attendants. However, the injuries were slight, and he was released from Carmarthen Hospital after a few days.

With the burial of Thomas and 'Babs', one would think that the story ended there, but shortly after his death, it was revealed that he had endowed a cot in the Great Ormond Street Hospital for Sick Children, at a cost of £50, the money coming partly from a B.B.C. broadcasting fee, and partly from a payment for exhibiting 'Babs' in Selfridges. With mass press coverage, a fund was set up to keep the 'Babs' cot in perpetuity, as a tribute to Thomas's memory. Interestingly, the largest single private donation was the sum of £20, from Miss Barbara Cooper - whether this lady had anything to do with the naming of 'Babs' can only be conjectured.

Moments after the awful tragedy. Jock Pullen is using a hand-held fire extinguisher on the still smouldering wreckage, whilst off camera to the right of the three men lay Thomas' body, covered by an overcoat. The arc of the car's track can clearly be seen in the background and foreground.

(Photograph by courtesy of Mrs. Betty Jones, nee Ebsworth)

42 years after Thomas' death, 'Babs' is exhumed from her resting place by Owen Wyn-Owen. The remarkable state of preservation of the car is clearly seen in the photograph.
(Photograph: Courtesy of Mr. John Eacott)

Resurrection

With the terrific increase in the Land Speed Record speeds in the late 1920s and 1930s, Pendine saw its demise as a venue of international importance. With the outbreak of war, a vast slice of the beach was taken over by the Ministry of Defence for a firing range, and 'Babs' grave was surrounded by buildings. Still, she lay undisturbed and over the years, forgotten by the Army staff, so much so that there was great surprise when, during excavations for an electricity cable, she was partly uncovered. After a few curious looks from those interested, she was re-covered and forgotten again.

It is at this point that the story takes a new twist; Owen Wyn-Owen, an engineering lecturer at Bangor Technical College, had a keen interest in vintage cars, and had already restored a Bentley, and a 1908 Argyll. One night, whilst chatting in a pub with friends, he said that he would like to try and find 'Babs', in the hope of digging her up, and restoring her to her former glory. The idea was not new; many other people had given thought to resurrecting 'Babs', but were deterred by Army red tape, and advice from those in the know that she would be hopelessly corroded.

Owen was not to be deterred, and in 1969, after much wrangling with the Army, and after being faced with local petitions for and against disturbing the car, he finally received permission to dig up 'Babs'. After the sand and mud had been washed away, observers were amazed at the condition of the car, which had lain virtually undisturbed for forty-two years. Only after 'Babs' had been taken to Owen's workshop at Capel Curig, could the full extent of the damage be seen. The frame was bent, almost all the aluminium components had corroded, including the gearbox casing and clutch bearing housing, the Zenith carburettors needed new chokes, and the engine camshafts were damaged beyond repair. British industry gallantly came to the rescue, with help coming from many sources, including rebuilding the gearbox, carburettors, radiator core and clutch. Dunlop provided new tyres, and a Liberty aero engine was donated by a retired naval officer, who had used it in a motor boat, the purpose of which was to avoid the police and customs officers in the U.S.A. in the days of Prohibition! A major obstacle which had to be overcome before 'Babs' could be run, was finding new drive chains. The original chains were of a pitch that was no longer made, but after much world wide detective work, replacements were found in Germany. In recent years, work has been concentrated on the body panels, and now wheel discs have been made, the long job is all but complete.

After fifteen years of hard work, 'Babs' is now restored to her former glory, and she is a regular sight at rallies and car shows. She has even returned to her two homes, Brooklands and Pendine. No finer tribute could be made to the memory of one of the greatest and most courageous racing drivers - Parry Thomas.

Acknowledgements

Grateful thanks are due to the following people for their kind assistance in producing this book:-

CLIFF REOHORN of the Beach Hotel, Pendine, for the loan of photographs from his fine collection.

JOE FREEMAN, who copied the photographs.

JIM CONNOR and BARBARA BUTLER for typesetting, graphics, and technical assistance.

JKL ADVERTISING & DESIGN for artwork.

OWEN WYN-OWEN.

TREVOR ISAACS.

DAFYDD PRICE, and the rest of the members of The Pendine Community Council.

R.H.BEAUCHAMP C.Eng.M.I.Mech E. Mr.Beauchamp worked for Thomas and later with Thomson and Taylor Ltd., and has provided valuable information.

Bibliography

PARRY THOMAS DESIGNER DRIVER by Hugh Tours.
(Pub: B.T.Batsford)
Long out of Print and very collectable, but indispensable reading for anyone interested in Parry Thomas.

THE HISTORY OF BROOKLANDS MOTOR COURSE by W.Boddy.
(Pub: Grenville Publishing Company Ltd. 1957)
The definitive book on Brooklands.

THE GLASS LADDER by June.
(Pub: Heinemann 1960)
The 'twenties musical comedy star who knew Thomas well.

FASTEST ON EARTH by Capt. G.E.T.Eyston
(Pub: John Miles Ltd. 1939)
The history of the World's Land Speed Record by the man who broke the record on three occasions.

THE AUTOMOBILE MAGAZINE October 1983 issue.
Article: 'The Resurrection of Babs' by 'The Prowler'.